DR. FAUSTUS

By Christopher Marlowe

A Digireads.com Book
Digireads.com Publishing
16212 Riggs Rd
Stilwell, KS, 66085

Dr. Faustus
By Christopher Marlowe
ISBN: 1-4209-2586-5

Introductory Note

CHRISTOPHER MARLOWE, the author of the earliest dramatic version of the Faust legend, was the son of a shoemaker in Canterbury, where he was born in February, 1564, some two months before Shakespeare. After graduating as M.A. from the University of Cambridge in 1587, he seems to have settled in London; and that same year is generally accepted as the latest date for the production of his tragedy of "Tamburlaine," the play which is regarded as having established blank verse as the standard meter of the English Drama. "Doctor Faustus" probably came next in 1588, followed by "The Jew of Malta" and "Edward II." Marlowe had a share in the production of several other plays, wrote the first two sestiads of "Hero and Leander," and made translations from Ovid and Lucan. He met his death in a tavern brawl, June 1, 1593.

Of Marlowe personally little is known. The common accounts of his atheistical beliefs and dissipated life are probably exaggerated, recent researches having given ground for believing that his heterodoxy may have amounted to little more than a form of Unitarianism. Some of the attacks on his character are based on the evidence of witnesses whose reputation will not bear investigation, while the character of some of his friends and their manner of speaking of him are of weight on the other side.

The most striking feature of Marlowe's dramas is the concentration of interest on an impressive central figure dominated by a single passion, the thirst for the unattainable. In "Tamburlaine" this takes the form of universal power; in "The Jew of Malta," infinite riches; in "Doctor Faustus" universal knowledge. The aspirations of these dominant personalities are uttered in sonorous blank verse, and in a rhetoric which at times rises to the sublime, at times descends to rant. "Doctor Faustus," though disfigured by poor comic scenes for which Marlowe is probably not responsible, and though lacking unity of structure, yet presents the career and fate of the hero with great power, and contains in the speech to Helen of Troy and in the dying utterance of Faustus two of the most superb passages of poetry in the English language.

Dramatis Personæ

[THE POPE. CARDINAL OF LORRAIN. EMPEROR OF
GERMANY.
DUKE OF VANHOLT. FAUSTUS.
VALDES and CORNELIUS, Friends to Faustus.
WAGNER, Servant to FAUSTUS.

Clown. ROBIN. RALPH.
Vintner, Horse-Courser, Knight, Old Man, Scholars, Friars,
and Attendants.

DUCHESS OF VANHOLT.

LUCIFER. BELZEBUB. MEPHISOPHILIS.

Good Angel, Evil Angel, The Seven Deadly Sins, Devils,
Spirits in the shape of ALEXANDER THE GREAT, of his
Paramour, and of HELEN OF TROY.
Chorus.]

Chorus

Enter CHORUS

Chorus. Not marching now in fields of Trasimene,
Where Mars did mate [1] the Carthaginians;
Nor sporting in the dalliance of love,
In courts of kings where state is overturn'd;
Nor in the pomp of proud audacious deeds,
Intends our Muse to vaunt his heavenly verse:
Only this, gentlemen,—we must perform
The form of Faustus' fortunes, good or bad.
To patient judgments we appeal our plaud, [2]
And speak for Faustus in his infancy.
Now is he born, his parents base of stock,
In Germany, within a town call'd Rhodes; [3]
Of riper years to Wittenberg he went,
Whereas his kinsmen chiefly brought him up.
So soon he profits in divinity,
The fruitful plot of scholarism grac'd, [4]
That shortly he was grac'd with doctor's name,
Excelling all those sweet delight disputes
In heavenly matters of theology;
Till swollen with cunning, [5] of a self-conceit,
His waxen wings [6] did mount above his reach,
And, melting, Heavens conspir'd his overthrow;
For, falling to a devilish exercise,
And glutted [now] with learning's golden gifts,
He surfeits upon cursed necromancy.
Nothing so sweet as magic is to him,
Which he prefers before his chiefest bliss.
And this the man that in his study sits! [*Exit.*]

[1] Confound. But Hannibal was victorious at Lake Trasimenus, B. C. 217.

[2] For applause.

[3] Roda, in the Duchy of Saxe-Altenburg, near Jena.

[4] The garden of scholarship being adorned by him.

[5] Knowledge.

[6] An allusion to the myth of Icarus, who flew too near the sun.

Scene I

FAUSTUS [*discovered*] *in his Study*

Faust. Settle my studies, Faustus, and begin
To sound the depth of that thou wilt profess; [1]
Having commenc'd, be a divine in show,
Yet level [2] and at the end of every art,
And live and die in Aristotle's works.
Sweet Analytics, [3] 'tis thou hast ravish'd me,
Bene disserere est finis logices. [4]
Is to dispute well logic's chiefest end?
Affords this art no greater miracle?
Then read no more, thou hast attain'd the end;
A greater subject fitteth Faustus' wit.
Bid ὄν καίμή ὄν [5] farewell; Galen come,
Seeing *Ubi desinit Philosophus ibi incipit Medicus*; [6]
Be a physician, Faustus, heap up gold,
And be eternis'd for some wondrous cure.
Summum bonum medicinæ sanitas, [7]
"The end of physic is our body's health"
Why, Faustus, hast thou not attain'd that end!
Is not thy common talk sound Aphorisms? [8]
Are not thy bills [9] hung up as monuments,
Whereby whole cities have escap'd the plague,
And thousand desperate maladies been eas'd?
Yet art thou still but Faustus and a man.
Couldst thou make men to live eternally,
Or, being dead, raise them to life again,
Then this profession were to be esteem'd.
Physic, farewell.—Where is Justinian? [*Reads.*]
*Si una eademque res legatur duobus, alter rem, alter
valorem rei, &c.* [10]
A pretty case of paltry legacies! [*Reads.*]

Ex hæreditare filium non potest pater nisi, &c. [11]
Such is the subject of the Institute [12]
And universal Body of the Law. [13]
His [14] study fits a mercenary drudge,
Who aims at nothing but external trash;
Too servile and illiberal for me.
When all is done, divinity is best;
Jerome's Bible, [15] Faustus, view it well. [*Reads.*]
Stipendium peccati mors est. Ha! *Stipendium, &c.*
"The reward of sin is death." That's hard. [*Reads.*]
Si peccasse negamus fallimur et nulla est in nobis veritas.
"If we say that we have no sin we deceive ourselves, and
    there's no truth in us." Why then, belike we must sin
    and so consequently die.
Ay, we must die an everlasting death.
What doctrine call you this, *Che sera sera,*
"What will be shall be?" Divinity, adieu
These metaphysics of magicians
And necromantic books are heavenly;
Lines, circles, scenes, letters, and characters,
Ay, these are those that Faustus most desires.
O what a world of profit and delight,
Of power, of honour, of omnipotence
Is promised to the studious artisan!
All things that move between the quiet poles
Shall be at my command. Emperor and kings
Are but obeyed in their several provinces,
Nor can they raise the wind or rend the clouds;
But his dominion that exceeds [16] in this
Stretcheth as far as doth the mind of man.
A sound magician is a mighty god:
Here, Faustus, try thy [17] brains to gain a deity.
Wagner!

Enter WAGNER

Commend me to my dearest friends,
The German Valdes and Cornelius;
Request them earnestly to visit me.

Wag. I will, sir. Exit.

Faust. Their conference will be a greater help to me
Than all my labours, plod I ne'er so fast.

Enter GOOD ANGEL *and* EVIL ANGEL

G. Ang. O Faustus! lay that damned book aside,
And gaze not upon it lest it tempt thy soul,
And heap God's heavy wrath upon thy head.
Read, read the Scriptures: that is blasphemy.

E. Ang. Go forward, Faustus, in that famous art,
Wherein all Nature's treasure is contain'd:
Be thou on earth as Jove is in the sky,
Lord and commander of these elements. [*Exeunt Angels.*]

Faust. How am I glutted with conceit [18] of this!
Shall I make spirits fetch me what I please,
Resolve me of all ambiguities,
Perform what desperate enterprise I will?
I'll have them fly to India for gold,
Ransack the ocean for orient pearl,
And search all corners of the new-found world
For pleasant fruits and princely delicates;
I'll have them read me strange philosophy
And tell the secrets of all foreign kings;
I'll have them wall all Germany with brass,
And make swift Rhine circle fair Wittenberg;
I'll have them fill the public schools with silk, [19]
Wherewith the students shall be bravely clad;

I'll levy soldiers with the coin they bring,
And chase the Prince of Parma from our land, [20]
And reign sole king of all the provinces;
Yea, stranger engines for the brunt of war
Than was the fiery keel [21] at Antwerp's bridge,
I'll make my servile spirits to invent.

Enter VALDES *and* CORNELIUS [22]

Come, German Valdes and Cornelius,
And make me blest with your sage conference.
Valdes, sweet Valdes, and Cornelius,
Know that your words have won me at the last
To practise magic and concealed arts:
Yet not your words only, but mine own fantasy
That will receive no object, for my head
But ruminates on necromantic skill.
Philosophy is odious and obscure,
Both law and physic are for petty wits;
Divinity is basest of the three,
Unpleasant, harsh, contemptible, and vile:
'Tis magic, magic, that hath ravish'd me.
Then, gentle friends, aid me in this attempt;
And I that have with concise syllogisms
Gravell'd the pastors of the German church,
And made the flowering pride of Wittenberg
Swarm to my problems, as the infernal spirits
On sweet Musæus, [23] when he came to hell,
Will be as cunning as Agrippa was,
Whose shadows made all Europe honour him.

Vald. Faustus, these books, thy wit, and our experience
Shall make all nations to canònise us.
As Indian Moors [24] obey their Spanish lords,
So shall the subjects [25] of every element

Be always serviceable to us three;
Like lions shall they guard us when we please;
Like Almain rutters [26] with their horsemen's staves
Or Lapland giants, trotting by our sides;
Sometimes like women or unwedded maids,
Shadowing more beauty in their airy brows
Than have the white breasts of the queen of love:
From Venice shall they drag huge argosies,
And from America the golden fleece
That yearly stuffs old Philip's treasury;
If learned Faustus will be resolute.

Faust. Valdes, as resolute am I in this
As thou to live; therefore object is not.

Corn. The miracles that magic will perform
Will make thee vow to study nothing else.
He that is grounded in astrology,
Enrich'd with tongues, as well seen [27] in minerals,
Hath all the principles magic doth require.
Then doubt not, Faustus, but to be renown'd,
And more frequented for this mystery
Than heretofore the Delphian Oracle.
The spirits tell me they can dry the sea,
And fetch the treasure of all foreign wrecks,
Ay, all the wealth that our forefathers hid
Within the massy entrails of the earth;
Then tell me, Faustus, what shall we three want?

Faust. Nothing, Cornelius! O this cheers my soul!
Come show me some demonstrations magical,
That I may conjure in some lusty grove,
And have these joys in full possession.

Vald. Then haste thee to some solitary grove,
And bear wise Bacon's [28] and Albanus' [29] works,
The Hebrew Psalter and New Testament;
And whatsoever else is requisite
We will inform thee ere our conference cease.

Corn. Valdes, first let him know the words of art;
And then, all other ceremonies learn'd,
Faustus may try his cunning by himself.

Vald. First I'll instruct thee in the rudiments,
And then wilt thou be perfecter than I.

Faust. Then come and dine with me, and after meat,
We'll canvass every quiddity thereof;
For ere I sleep I'll try what I can do:
This night I'll conjure though I die therefore. [*Exeunt.*]

[1] Teach publicly.
[2] Aim.
[3] Logic.
[4] "To argue well is the end of logic."
[5] This is Mr. Bullen's emendation of Q1., Oncaymæon, a corruption of the Aristotelian phrase for "being and not being."
[6] "Where the philosopher leaves off, there the physician begins."
[7] This and the previous quotation are from Aristotle.
[8] Medical maxims.
[9] Announcements.
[10] "If one and the same thing is bequeathed to two person, one gets the thing and the other the value of the thing."
[11] "A father cannot disinherit the son except," etc.

[12] Of Justinian, under whom the Roman law was codified.

[13] Q1., Church.

[14] Its.

[15] The Vulgate.

[16] Excels.

[17] Q3., tire my.

[18] Idea.

[19] Qq., skill.

[20] The Netherlands, over which Parma re-established the Spanish dominions.

[21] A ship filled with explosives used to blow up a bridge built by Parma in 1585 at the siege of Antwerp.

[22] The famous Cornelius Agrippa. German Valdes is not known.

[23] Cf. Virgil, *Æn.* vi. 667; Dryden's trans. vi. 905 ff.

[24] American Indians.

[25] Q3., spirits.

[26] Troopers, Germ. *Reiters.*

[27] Versed.

[28] Roger Bacon.

[29] Perhaps Pietro d'Abano, a medieval alchemist; perhaps a misprint for Albertus (Magnus), the great schoolman.

Scene II

[*Before* FAUSTUS'S *House*]
Enter two SCHOLARS

1st Schol. I wonder what's become of Faustus that was wont to make our schools ring with *sic probo*? [1]

2nd Schol. That shall we know, for see here comes his boy.

Enter WAGNER

1st Schol. How now, sirrah! Where's thy master?

Wag. God in heaven knows!

2nd Schol. Why, dost not thou know?

Wag. Yes, I know. But that follows not.

1st Schol. Go to, sirrah! Leave your jesting, and tell us where he is.

Wag. That follows not necessary by force of argument, that you, being licentiate, should stand upon't: therefore, acknowledge your error and be attentive.

2nd Schol. Why, didst thou not say thou knew'st?

Wag. Have you any witness on't?

1st Schol. Yes, sirrah, I heard you.

Wag. Ask my fellow if I be a thief.

2nd Schol. Well, you will not tell us?

Wag. Yes, sir, I will tell you; yet if you were not dunces, you would never ask me such a question; for is not he *corpus naturale*? [2] and is not that *mobile*? Then wherefore should you ask me such a question? But that I am by nature phlegmatic, slow to wrath, and prone to lechery (to love, I would say), it were not for you to come within forty feet of the place of execution, although I do not doubt to see you both hang'd the next sessions. Thus having triumph'd over you, I will set my countenance like a precisian, [3] and begin to speak thus:—Truly, my dear brethren, my master is within at dinner, with Valdes and Cornelius, as this wine, if it could speak, would inform your worships; and so the Lord bless you, preserve you, and keep you, my dear brethren, my dear brethren.

1st Schol. Nay, then, I fear he has fallen into that damned Art, for which they two are infamous through the world.

2nd Schol. Were he a stranger, and not allied to me, yet should I grieve for him. But come, let us go and inform the Rector, and see if he by his grave counsel can reclaim him.

1st Schol. O, but I fear me nothing can reclaim him.

2nd Schol. Yet let us try what we can do. [*Exeunt.*]

[1] "Thus I prove"—a common formula in scholastic discussions.

[2] "*'Corpus naturale seu mobile'* is the current scholastic expression for the subject-matter of physics."—Ward.

[3] Puritan.

Scene III

[A Grove.]
Enter FAUSTUS *to conjure*

Faust. Now that the gloomy shadow of the earth
Longing to view Orion's drizzling look,
Leaps from the antarctic world unto the sky,
And dims the welkin with her pitchy breath,
Faustus, begin thine incantations,
And try if devils will obey thy hest,
Seeing thou hast pray'd and sacrific'd to them.
Within this circle is Jehovah's name,
Forward and backward anagrammatis'd,
The breviated names of holy saints,
Figures of every adjunct to the Heavens,
And characters of signs and erring [1] stars,
By which the spirits are enforc'd to rise:
Then fear not, Faustus, but be resolute,
And try the uttermost magic can perform.
*Sint mihi Dei Acherontis propitii! Valeat numen triplex
Jehovae! Ignei, aerii, aquatani spiritus, salvete!
Orientis princeps Belzebub, inferni ardentis monarcha,
et Demogorgon, propitiamus vos, ut appareat et surgat
Mephistophilis. Quid tu moraris? per Jehovam,
Gehennam et consecratum aquam quam nunc spargo,
signumque crucis quod nunc facio, et per vota nostra,
ipse nunc surgat nobis dicatus Mephistophilis!* [2]

Enter [MEPHISTOPHILIS] *a* DEVIL

I charge thee to return and change thy shape;
Thou art too ugly to attend on me.
Go, and return an old Franciscan friar;

That holy shape becomes a devil best. [*Exit* DEVIL]
I see there's virtue in my heavenly words;
Who would not be proficient in this art?
How pliant is this Mephistophilis,
Full of obedience and humility!
Such is the force of magic and my spells.
[Now,] Faustus, thou art conjuror laureat,
Thou canst command great Mephistophilis:
Quin regis Mephistophilis fratris imagine. [3]

Re-enter MEPHISTOPHILIS [*like a Franciscan Friar*]

Meph. Now, Faustus, what would'st thou have me to do?

Faust. I charge thee wait upon me whilst I live,
To do whatever Faustus shall command,
Be it to make the moon drop from her sphere,
Or the ocean to overwhelm the world.

Meph. I am a servant to great Lucifer,
And may not follow thee without his leave
No more than he commands must we perform.

Faust. Did not he charge thee to appear to me?

Meph. No, I came hither of mine own accord.

Faust. Did not my conjuring speeches raise thee? Speak.

Meph. That was the cause, but yet *per accidens*;
For when we hear one rack [4] the name of God,
Abjure the Scriptures and his Saviour Christ,
We fly in hope to get his glorious soul;
Nor will we come, unless he use such means
Whereby he is in danger to be damn'd:

Therefore the shortest cut for conjuring
Is stoutly to abjure the Trinity,
And pray devoutly to the Prince of Hell.

Faust. So Faustus hath
Already done; and holds this principle,
There is no chief but only Belzebub,
To whom Faustus doth dedicate himself.
This word "damnation" terrifies not him,
For he confounds hell in Elysium; [5]
His ghost be with the old philosophers!
But, leaving these vain trifles of men's souls,
Tell me what is that Lucifer thy lord?

Meph. Arch-regent and commander of all spirits.

Faust. Was not that Lucifer an angel once?

Meph. Yes, Faustus, and most dearly lov'd of God.

Faust. How comes it then that he is Prince of devils?

Meph. O, by aspiring pride and insolence;
For which God threw him from the face of Heaven.

Faust. And what are you that you live with Lucifer?

Meph. Unhappy spirits that fell with Lucifer,
Conspir'd against our God with Lucifer,
And are for ever damn'd with Lucifer.

Faust. Where are you damn'd?

Meph. In hell.

Faust. How comes it then that thou art out of hell?

Meph. Why this is hell, nor am I out of it.
Think'st thou that I who saw the face of God,
And tasted the eternal joys of Heaven,
Am not tormented with ten thousand hells,
In being depriv'd of everlasting bliss?
O Faustus! leave these frivolous demands,
Which strike a terror to my fainting soul.

Faust. What, is great Mephistophilis so passionate
For being depriv'd of the joys of Heaven?
Learn thou of Faustus manly fortitude,
And scorn those joys thou never shalt possess.
Go bear these tidings to great Lucifer:
Seeing Faustus hath incurr'd eternal death
By desperate thoughts against Jove's deity,
Say he surrenders up to him his soul,
So he will spare him four and twenty years,
Letting him live in all voluptuousness;
Having thee ever to attend on me;
To give me whatsoever I shall ask,
To tell me whatsoever I demand,
To slay mine enemies, and aid my friends,
And always be obedient to my will.
Go and return to mighty Lucifer,
And meet me in my study at midnight,
And then resolve [6] me of thy master's mind.

Meph. I will, Faustus. [*Exit.*]

Faust. Had I as many souls as there be stars,
I'd give them all for Mephistophilis.
By him I'll be great Emperor of the world,
And make a bridge through the moving air,

To pass the ocean with a band of men:
I'll join the hills that bind the Afric shore,
And make that [country] continent to Spain,
And both contributory to my crown.
The Emperor shall not live but by my leave,
Nor any potentate of Germany.
Now that I have obtain'd what I desire,
I'll live in speculation [7] of this art
Till Mephistophilis return again. [*Exit.*]

[1] Wandering.
[2] "Be propitious to me, gods of Acheron! May the triple deity of Jehovah prevail! Spirits of fire, air, water, hail! Belzebub, Prince of the East, monarch of burning hell, and Demogorgon, we propitiate ye, that Mephistophilis may appear and rise. Why dost thou delay? By Jehovah, Gehenna, and the holy water which now I sprinkle, and the sign of the cross which now I make, and by our prayer, may Mephistophilis now summoned by us arise!"
[3] "For indeed thou hast power in the image of thy brother Mephistophilis."
[4] Twist in anagrams.
[5] Heaven and hell are indifferent to him.
[6] Inform.
[7] Study.

Scene IV

[A Street.]
Enter WAGNER *and* CLOWN

Wag. Sirrah, boy, come hither.

Clown. How, boy! Swowns, [1] boy! I hope you have seen many boys with such pickadevaunts [2] as I have. Boy, quotha!

Wag. Tell me, sirrah, hast thou any comings in?

Clown. Ay, and goings out too. You may see else.

Wag. Alas, poor slave! See how poverty jesteth in his nakedness! The villain is bare and out of service, and so hungry that I know he would give his soul to the devil for a shoulder of mutton, though it were blood-raw.

Clown. How? My soul to the Devil for a shoulder of mutton, though 'twere blood-raw! Not so, good friend. By'r Lady, I had need have it well roasted and good sauce to it, if I pay so dear.

Wag. Well, wilt thou serve me, and I'll make thee go like *Qui mihi discipulus*? [3]

Clown. How, in verse?

Wag. No, sirrah; in beaten silk and stavesacre. [4]

Clown. How, how, Knave's acre! [5] Ay, I thought that was all the land his father left him. Do you hear? I would be sorry to rob you of your living.

Wag. Sirrah, I say in stavesacre.

Clown. Oho! Oho! Stavesacre! Why, then, belike if I were your man I should be full of vermin.

Wag. So thou shalt, whether thou beest with me or no. But, sirrah, leave your jesting, and bind yourself presently unto me for seven years, or I'll turn all the lice about thee into familiars, and they shall tear thee in pieces.

Clown. Do your hear, sir? You may save that labour; they are too familiar with me already. Swowns! they are as bold with my flesh as if they had paid for [their] meat and drink.

Wag. Well, do you hear, sirrah? Hold, take these guilders. [*Gives money.*]

Clown. Gridirons! what be they?

Wag. Why, French crowns.

Clown. Mass, but for the name of French crowns, a man were as good have as many English counters. And what should I do with these?

Wag. Why, now, sirrah, thou art at an hour's warning, whensoever and wheresoever the Devil shall fetch thee.

Clown. No, no. Here, take your gridirons again.

Wag. Truly I'll none of them.

Clown. Truly but you shall.

Wag. Bear witness I gave them him.

Clown. Bear witness I gave them you again.

Wag. Well, I will cause two devils presently to fetch thee away—Baliol and Belcher.

Clown. Let your Baliol and your Belcher come here, and I'll knock them, they were never so knock'd since they were devils. Say I should kill one of them, what would folks say? "Do you see yonder tall fellow in the round slop [6] —he has kill'd the devil." So I should be called Kill-devil all the parish over.

Enter two Devils: *the* Clown *runs up and down crying*

Wag. Baliol and Belcher! Spirits, away! [*Exeunt* Devils.]

Clown. What, are they gone? A vengeance on them, they have vile long nails! There was a he-devil, and a she-devil! I'll tell you how you shall know them: all he-devils has horns, and all she-devils has clifts and cloven feet.

Wag. Well, sirrah, follow me.

Clown. But, do you hear—if I should serve you, would you teach me to raise up Banios and Belcheos?

Wag. I will teach thee to turn thyself to anything; to a dog, or a cat, or a mouse, or a rat, or anything.

Clown. How! a Christian fellow to a dog or a cat, a mouse or a rat! No, no, sir. If you turn me into anything, let it be in the likeness of a little pretty frisky flea, that I may be here and there and everywhere. Oh, I'll tickle the pretty wenches' plackets; I'll be amongst them, i' faith.

Wag. Well, sirrah, come.

Clown. But, do you hear, Wagner?

Wag. How! Baliol and Belcher!

Clown. O Lord! I pray, sir, let Banio and Belcher go sleep.

Wag. Villain—call me Master Wagner, and let thy left eye be diametarily [7] fixed upon my right heel, with *quasi vestigias nostras insistere.* [8] [*Exit.*]

Clown. God forgive me, he speaks Dutch fustian. Well, I'll follow him, I'll serve him, that's flat. [*Exit.*]

[1] Zounds, i. e., God's wounds.
[2] Beards cut to a sharp point (Fr. *pic-à-devant*).
[3] Dyce points out that these are the first words of W. Lily's "*Ad discipulos carmen de moribus.*"
[4] A kind of larkspur, used for destroying lice.
[5] A mean street in London.
[6] Short wide breeches.
[7] For diametrically.
[8] "As if to tread in my tracks."

Scene V

FAUSTUS [*discovered*] *in his Study*

Faust. Now, Faustus, must
Thou needs be damn'd, and canst thou not be sav'd:
What boots it then to think of God or Heaven?
Away with such vain fancies, and despair:
Despair in God, and trust in Belzebub.
Now go not backward: no, Faustus, be resolute.
Why waverest thou? O, something soundeth in mine ears
"Abjure this magic, turn to God again!"
Ay, and Faustus will turn to God again.
To God?—He loves thee not—
The God thou serv'st is thine own appetite,
Wherein is fix'd the love of Belzebub;
To him I'll build an altar and a church,
And offer lukewarm blood of new-born babes.

Enter GOOD ANGEL *and* EVIL ANGEL

G. Ang. Sweet Faustus, leave that execrable art.

Faust. Contrition, prayer, repentance! What of them?

G. Ang. O, they are means to bring thee unto Heaven.

E. Ang. Rather, illusions, fruits of lunacy,
That makes men foolish that do trust them most.

G. Ang. Sweet Faustus, think of Heaven, and heavenly
    things.

E. Ang. No, Faustus, think of honour and of wealth.
  [*Exeunt* ANGELS.]

Faust. Of wealth!
What the signiory of Embden [1] shall be mine.
When Mephistophilis shall stand by me,
What God can hurt thee, Faustus? Thou art safe;
Cast no more doubts. Come, Mephistophilis,
And bring glad tidings from great Lucifer;—
Is't not midnight? Come, Mephistophilis;
Veni, veni, Mephistophile!

Enter MEPHISTOPHILIS

Now tell me, what says Lucifer thy lord?

Meph. That I shall wait on Faustus whilst he lives,
So he will buy my service with his soul.

Faust. Already Faustus hath hazarded that for thee.

Meph. But, Faustus, thou must bequeath it solemnly,
And write a deed of gift with thine own blood,
For that security craves great Lucifer.
If thou deny it, I will back to hell.

Faust. Stay, Mephistophilis! and tell me what good
Will my soul do thy lord.

Meph. Enlarge his kingdom.

Faust. Is that the reason why he tempts us thus?

Meph. Solamen miseris socios habuisse doloris. [2]

Faust. Why, have you any pain that torture others?

Meph. As great as have the human souls of men.
But tell me, Faustus, shall I have thy soul?
And I will be thy slave, and wait on thee,
And give thee more than thou hast wit to ask.

Faust. Ay, Mephistophilis, I give it thee.

Meph. Then, Faustus, stab thine arm courageously.
And bind thy soul that at some certain day
Great Lucifer may claim it as his own;
And then be thou as great as Lucifer.

Faust. [*stabbing his arm.*] Lo, Mephistophilis, for love of
    thee,
I cut mine arm, and with my proper blood
Assure my soul to be great Lucifer's,
Chief lord and regent of perpetual night!
View here the blood that trickles from mine arm.
And let it be propitious for my wish.

Meph. But, Faustus, thou must
Write it in manner of a deed of gift.

Faust. Ay, so I will. [*Writes.*] But, Mephistophilis,
My blood congeals, and I can write no more.

Meph. I'll fetch thee fire to dissolve it straight. [*Exit.*]

Faust. What might the staying of my blood portend?
Is it unwilling I should write this bill?
Why streams it not that I may write afresh?
Faustus gives to thee his soul. Ah, there it stay'd.
Why should'st thou not? Is not thy soul thine own?

Then write again. *Faustus gives to thee his soul.*

Re-enter MEPHISTOPHILIS *with a chafer of coals*

Meph. Here's fire. Come, Faustus, set it on.

Faust. So now the blood begins to clear again;
Now will I make an end immediately. [*Writes.*]

Meph. O what will not I do to obtain his soul. [*Aside.*]

Faust. Consummatum est: [3] this bill is ended,
And Faustus hath bequeath'd his soul to Lucifer—
But what is this inscription on mine arm?
Homo, fuge! [4] Whither should I fly?
If unto God, he'll throw me down to hell.
My senses are deceiv'd; here's nothing writ:—
I see it plain; here in this place is writ
Homo, fuge! Yet shall not Faustus fly.

Meph. I'll fetch him somewhat to delight his mind. [*Exit.*]

Re-enter [MEPHISTOPHILIS] *with* Devils, *giving crowns
and rich apparel to* FAUSTUS, *dance, and depart*

Faust. Speak Mephistophilis, what means this show?

Meph. Nothing, Faustus, but to delight thy mind withal,
And to show thee what magic can perform.

Faust. But may I raise up spirits when I please?

Meph. Ay, Faustus, and do greater things than these.

Faust. Then there's enough for a thousand souls.

Here, Mephistophilis, receive this scroll,
A deed of gift of body and of soul:
But yet conditionally that thou perform
All articles prescrib'd between us both.

Meph. Faustus, I swear by hell and Lucifer
To effect all promises between us made.

Faust. Then hear me read them: *On these conditions following. First, that Faustus may be a spirit in form and substance. Secondly, that Mephistophilis shall be his servant, and at his command. Thirdly, that Mephistophilis shall do for him and bring him whatsoever [he desires]. Fourthly, that he shall be in his chamber or house invisible. Lastly, that he shall appear to the said John Faustus, at all times, and in what form or shape soever he pleases. I, John Faustus, of Wittenberg, Doctor, by these presents do give both body and soul to Lucifer, Prince of the East, and his minister, Mephistophilis; and furthermore grant unto them, that twenty-four years being expired, the articles above written inviolate, full power to fetch or carry the said John Faustus, body and soul, flesh, blood, or goods, into their habitation wheresoever. By me, John Faustus.*

Meph. Speak, Faustus, do you deliver this as your deed?

Faust. Ay, take it, and the Devil give thee good on't.

Meph. Now, Faustus, ask what thou wilt.

Faust. First will I question with thee about hell.
Tell me where is the place that men call hell?

Meph. Under the Heaven.

Faust. Ay, but whereabout?

Meph. Within the bowels of these elements,
Where we are tortur'd and remain for ever;
Hell hath no limits, nor is circumscrib'd
In one self place; for where we are is hell,
And where hell is there must we ever be:
And, to conclude, when all the world dissolves,
And every creature shall be purified,
All places shall be hell that is not Heaven.

Faust. Come, I think hell's a fable.

Meph. Ay, think so still, till experience change thy mind.

Faust. Why, think'st thou then that Faustus shall be
    damn'd?

Meph. Ay, of necessity, for here's the scroll
Wherein thou hast given thy soul to Lucifer.

Faust. Ay, and body too; but what of that?
Think'st thou that Faustus is so fond [5] to imagine
That, after this life, there is any pain?
Tush; these are trifles, and mere old wives' tales.

Meph. But, Faustus, I am an instance to prove the contrary,
For I am damned, and am now in hell.

Faust. How! now in hell!
Nay, an this be hell, I'll willingly be damn'd here;
What? walking, disputing, &c.?
But, leaving off this, let me have a wife,

The fairest maid in Germany;
For I am wanton and lascivious,
And cannot live without a wife.

Meph. How—a wife?
I prithee, Faustus, talk not of a wife.

Faust. Nay, sweet Mephistophilis, fetch me one, for I will
    have one.

Meph. Well—thou wilt have one. Sit there till I come:
I'll fetch thee a wife in the Devil's name. [*Exit.*]

Re-enter MEPHISTOPHILIS *with a* DEVIL *dressed like a
woman, with fireworks*

Meph. Tell me, Faustus, how dost thou like thy wife?

Faust. A plague on her for a hot whore!

Meph. Tut, Faustus,
Marriage is but a ceremonial toy;
And if thou lovest me, think no more of it.
I'll cull thee out the fairest courtesans,
And bring them every morning to thy bed;
She whom thine eye shall like, thy heart shall have,
Be she as chaste as was Penelope,
As wise as Saba, [6] or as beautiful
As was bright Lucifer before his fall.
Here, take this book peruse it thoroughly: [*Gives a book.*]
The iterating [7] of these lines brings gold;
The framing of this circle on the ground
Brings whirlwinds, tempests, thunder and lightning;
Pronounce this thrice devoutly to thyself,
And men in armour shall appear to thee,

Ready to execute what thou desir'st.

Faust. Thanks, Mephistophilis; yet fain would I have a book wherein I might behold all spells and incantations, that I might raise up spirits when I please.

Meph. Here they are, in this book. [*Turns to them.*]

Faust. Now would I have a book where I might see all characters and planets of the heavens, that I might know their motions and dispositions.

Meph. Here they are too. [*Turns to them.*]

Faust. Nay, let me have one book more,—and then I have done,—wherein I might see all plants, herbs, and trees that grow upon the earth.

Meph. Here they be.

Faust. O, thou art deceived.

Meph. Tut, I warrant thee. [*Turns to them. Exeunt.*]

[1] Emden, near the mouth of the river Ems, was an important commercial town in Elizabethan times.
[2] "Misery loves company."
[3] "It is finished."
[4] "Man, fly!"
[5] Foolish.
[6] The Queen of Sheba.
[7] Repeating.

Scene VI

[The Same.]
Enter FAUSTUS *and* MEPHISTOPHILIS

Faust. When I behold the heavens, then I repent,
And curse thee, wicked Mephistophilis,
Because thou hast depriv'd me of those joys.

Meph. Why, Faustus,
Thinkest thou Heaven is such a glorious thing?
I tell thee 'tis not half so fair as thou,
Or any man that breathes on earth.

Faust. How provest thou that?

Meph. 'Twas made for man, therefore is man more
excellent.

Faust. If it were made for man, 'twas made for me:
I will renounce this magic and repent.

Enter GOOD ANGEL *and* EVIL ANGEL

G. Ang. Faustus, repent; yet God will pity thee.

E. Ang. Thou art a spirit; God can not pity thee.

Faust. Who buzzeth in mine ears I am a spirit?
Be I a devil, yet God may pity me;
Ay, God will pity me if I repent.

E. Ang. Ay, but Faustus never shall repent. [*Exeunt*
ANGELS.]

Faust. My heart's so hard'ned I cannot repent.
Scarce can I name salvation, faith, or heaven,
But fearful echoes thunder in mine ears
"Faustus, thou art damn'd!" Then swords and knives,
Poison, gun, halters, and envenom'd steel
Are laid before me to despatch myself,
And long ere this I should have slain myself,
Had not sweet pleasure conquer'd deep despair.
Have I not made blind Homer sing to me
Of Alexander's love and Œnon's death?
And hath not he that built the walls of Thebes
With ravishing sound of his melodious harp,
Made music with my Mephistophilis?
Why should I die then, or basely despair?
I am resolv'd: Faustus shall ne'er repent.
Come, Mephistophilis, let us dispute again,
And argue of divine astrology.
Tell me, are there many heavens above the moon?
Are all celestial bodies but one globe,
As is the substance of this centric earth?

Meph. As are the elements, such are the spheres
Mutually folded in each other's orb,
And, Faustus,
All jointly move upon one axletree
Whose terminine is termed the world's wide pole;
Nor are the names of Saturn, Mars, or Jupiter
Feign'd but are erring stars.

Faust. But tell me, have they all one motion, both *situ et tempore?* [1]

Meph. All jointly move from east to west in twenty-four hours upon the poles of the world; but differ in their motion upon the poles of the zodiac.

Faust. Tush!
These slender trifles Wagner can decide;
Hath Mephistophilis no greater skill?
Who knows not the double motion of the planets?
The first is finish'd in a natural day;
The second thus: as Saturn in thirty years; Jupiter in twelve; Mars in four; the Sun, Venus, and Mercury in a year; the moon in twenty-eight days. Tush, these are freshmen's suppositions. But tell me, hath every sphere a dominion or *intelligentia*?

Meph. Ay.

Faust. How many heavens, or spheres, are there?

Meph. Nine: the seven planets, the firmament, and the empyreal heaven.

Faust. Well, resolve me in this question: Why have we not conjunctions, oppositions, aspects, eclipses, all at one time, but in some years we have more, in some less?

Meph. Per inæqualem motum respectu totius. [2]

Faust. Well, I am answered. Tell me who made the world.

Meph. I will not.

Faust. Sweet Mephistophilis, tell me.

Meph. Move me not, for I will not tell thee.

Faust. Villain, have I not bound thee to tell me anything?

Meph. Ay, that is not against our kingdom; but this is.
Think thou on hell, Faustus, for thou art damn'd.

Faust. Think, Faustus, upon God that made the world.

Meph. Remember this.

Faust. Ay, go, accursed spirit, to ugly hell.
'Tis thou hast damn'd distressed Faustus' soul.
Is't not too late?

    Re-enter GOOD ANGEL *and* EVIL ANGEL.

E. Ang. Too late.

G. Ang. Never too late, if Faustus can repent.

E. Ang. If thou repent, devils shall tear thee in pieces.

G. Ang. Repent, and they shall never raze thy skin. [*Exeunt*
    ANGELS.]

Faust. Ah, Christ, my Saviour,
Seek to save distressed Faustus' soul.

   Enter LUCIFER, BELZEBUB, *and* MEPHISTOPHILIS.

Luc. Christ cannot save thy soul, for he is just;
There's none but I have interest in the same.

Faust. O, who art thou that look'st so terrible?

Luc. I am Lucifer,
And this is my companion-prince in hell.

Faust. O Faustus! they are come to fetch away thy soul!

Luc. We come to tell thee thou dost injure us;
Thou talk'st of Christ contrary to thy promise;
Thou should'st not think of God: think of the Devil,
And of his dam, too.

Faust. Nor will I henceforth: pardon me in this,
And Faustus vows never to look to Heaven,
Never to name God, or to pray to him,
To burn his Scriptures, slay his ministers,
And make my spirits pull his churches down.

Luc. Do so, and we will highly gratify thee. Faustus, we are
come from hell to show thee some pastime. Sit down,
and thou shalt see all the Seven Deadly Sins appear in
their proper shapes.

Faust. That sight will be as pleasing unto me,
As Paradise was to Adam the first day
Of his creation.

Luc. Talk not of Paradise nor creation, but mark this show:
talk of the Devil, and nothing else.—Come away!

Enter the SEVEN DEADLY SINS.

Now, Faustus, examine them of their several names and
dispositions.

Faust. What art thou—the first?

Pride. I am Pride. I disdain to have any parents. I am like to Ovid's flea: I can creep into every corner of a wench; sometimes, like a periwig, I sit upon her brow; or like a fan of feathers, I kiss her lips; indeed I do—what do I not? But, fie, what a scent is here! I'll not speak another word, except the ground were perfum'd, and covered with cloth of arras.

Faust. What art thou—the second?

Covet. I am Covetousness, begotten of an old churl in an old leathern bag; and might I have my wish I would desire that this house and all the people in it were turn'd to gold, that I might lock you up in my good chest. O, my sweet gold!

Faust. What art thou—the third?

Wrath. I am Wrath. I had neither father nor mother: I leapt out of a lion's mouth when I was scarce half an hour old; and ever since I have run up and down the world with this case [3] of rapiers, wounding myself when I had nobody to fight withal. I was born in hell; and look to it, for some of you shall be my father.

Faust. What art thou—the fourth?

Envy. I am Envy, begotten of a chimney sweeper and an oyster-wife. I cannot read, and therefore wish all books were burnt. I am lean with seeing others eat. O that there would come a famine through all the world, that all might die, and I live alone! then thou should'st see how fat I would be. But must thou sit and I stand! Come down with a vengeance!

Faust. Away, envious rascal! What art thou—the fifth?

Glut. Who, I, sir? I am Gluttony. My parents are all dead, and the devil a penny they have left me, but a bare pension, and that is thirty meals a day and ten bevers [4] —a small trifle to suffice nature. O, I come of a royal parentage! My grandfather was a Gammon of Bacon, my grandmother a Hogshead of Claret-wine; my godfathers were these, Peter Pickleherring, and Martin Martlemas-beef. [5] O, but my godmother, she was a jolly gentlewoman, and well beloved in every good town and city; her name was Mistress Margery Marchbeer. Now, Faustus, thou hast heard all my progeny, wilt thou bid me to supper?

Faust. No, I'll see thee hanged: thou wilt eat up all my victuals.

Glut. Then the Devil choke thee!

Faust. Choke thyself, glutton! Who art thou—the sixth?

Sloth. I am Sloth. I was begotten on a sunny bank, where I have lain ever since; and you have done me great injury to bring me from thence: let me be carried thither again by Gluttony and Lechery. I'll not speak another word for a king's ransom.

Faust. What are you, Mistress Minx, the seventh and last?

Lech. Who, I, sir? I am one that loves an inch of raw mutton better than an ell of fried stockfish; and the first letter of my name begins with Lechery.

Luc. Away to hell, to hell!—Now, Faustus, how dost thou
   like this? [*Exeunt the* SINS.]

Faust. O, this feeds my soul!

Luc. Tut, Faustus, in hell is all manner of delight.

Faust. O might I see hell, and return again,
How happy were I then!

Luc. Thou shalt; I will send for thee at midnight.
In meantime take this book; peruse it throughly,
And thou shalt turn thyself into what shape thou wilt.

Faust. Great thanks, mighty Lucifer!
This will I keep as chary as my life.

Luc. Farewell, Faustus, and think on the Devil.

Faust. Farewell, great Lucifer! Come, Mephistophilis.
   [*Exeunt.*]

Enter CHORUS

Chorus. Learned Faustus,
To know the secrets of astronomy,
Graven in the book of Jove's high firmament,
Did mount himself to scale Olympus' top,
Being seated in a chariot burning bright,
Drawn by the strength of yoky dragons' necks.
He now is gone to prove cosmography,
And, as I guess, will first arrive at Rome,
To see the Pope and manner of his court,
And take some part of holy Peter's feast,
That to this day is highly solemnis'd. [*Exit.*]

[1] "In direction and in time?"

[2] "On account of their unequal motion in relation to the whole."

[3] Pair.

[4] Refreshments between meals.

[5] Martlemas or Martinmas was "the customary time for hanging up provisions to dry which had been salted for the winter."—*Nares*.

Scene VII

[*The Pope's Privy-chamber.*]
Enter FAUSTUS *and* MEPHISTOPHILIS

Faust. Having now, my good Mephistophilis,
Passed with delight the stately town of Trier, [1]
Environ'd round with airy mountain-tops,
With walls of flint, and deep entrenched lakes,
Not to be won by any conquering prince;
From Paris next, coasting the realm of France,
We saw the river Maine fall into Rhine,
Whose banks are set with groves of fruitful vines;
Then up to Naples, rich Campania,
Whose buildings fair and gorgeous to the eye,
The streets straight forth, and pav'd with finest brick,
Quarter the town in four equivalents.
There saw we learned Maro's [2] golden tomb,
The way he cut, an English mile in length,
Thorough a rock of stone in one night's space;
From thence to Venice, Padua, and the rest,
In one of which a sumptuous temple stands,
That threats the stars with her aspiring top.
Thus hitherto has Faustus spent his time:
But tell me, now, what resting-place is this?
Hast thou, as erst I did command,
Conducted me within the walls of Rome?

Meph. Faustus, I have; and because we will not be
unprovided, I have taken up his Holiness' privy-
chamber for our use.

Faust. I hope his Holiness will bid us welcome.

Meph. Tut, 'tis no matter, man, we'll be bold with his good
    cheer.
And now, my Faustus, that thou may'st perceive
What Rome containeth to delight thee with,
Know that this city stands upon seven hills
That underprop the groundwork of the same.
[Just through the midst runs flowing Tiber's stream,
With winding banks that cut it in two parts:]
Over the which four stately bridges lean,
That make safe passage to each part of Rome:
Upon the bridge called Ponte Angelo
Erected is a castle passing strong,
Within whose walls such store of ordnance are,
And double cannons fram'd of carved brass,
As match the days within one complete year;
Besides the gates and high pyramides,
Which Julius Cæsar brought from Africa.

Faust. Now by the kingdoms of infernal rule,
Of Styx, of Acheron, and the fiery lake
Of ever-burning Phlegethon, I swear
That I do long to see the monuments
And situation of bright-splendent Rome:
Come therefore, let's away.

Meph. Nay, Faustus, stay: I know you'd see the Pope,
And take some part of holy Peter's feast,
Where thou shalt see a troop of bald-pate friars,
Whose *summum bonum* is in belly-cheer.

Faust. Well, I'm content to compass then some sport,
And by their folly make us merriment.
Then charm me, [Mephistophilis,] that I
May be invisible, to do what I please

Unseen of any whilst I stay in Rome. [MEPHISTOPHILIS
  charms him.]

Meph. So, Faustus, now
Do what thou wilt, thou shalt not be discern'd.

Sound a sennett. [3] *Enter the* POPE *and the* CARDINAL
  of LORRAIN *to the banquet, with* FRIARS *attending*

Pope. My Lord of Lorrain, wilt please you draw near?

Faust. Fall to, and the devil choke you an [4] you spare!

Pope. How now! Who's that which spake?—Friars, look
  about.

First Friar. Here's nobody, if it like your Holiness.

Pope. My lord, here is a dainty dish was sent me from the
  Bishop of Milan.

Faust. I thank you, sir. [*Snatches the dish.*]

Pope. How now! Who's that which snatched the meat from
  me? Will no man look? My lord, this dish was sent me
  from the Cardinal of Florence.

Faust. You say true; I'll ha't. [*Snatches the dish.*]

Pope. What, again! My lord, I'll drink to your Grace.

Faust. I'll pledge your Grace. [*Snatches the cup.*]

C. of Lor. My lord, it may be some ghost newly crept out of
  purgatory, come to beg a pardon of your Holiness.

Pope. It may be so. Friars, prepare a dirge to lay the fury of this ghost. Once again, my lord, fall to. [*The* POPE *crosses himself.*]

Faust. What, are you crossing of yourself?
Well, use that trick no more I would advise you.

        The POPE *crosses himself again.*

Well, there's the second time. Aware the third,
I give you fair warning.

    The POPE *crosses himself again, and Faustus hits him a
        box 'f the ear; and they all run away.*

Come on, Mephistophilis, what shall we do?

Meph. Nay, I know not. We shall be curs'd with bell, book, and candle.

Faust. How! bell, book, and candle,—candle, book, and bell,
Forward and backward to curse Faustus to hell!
Anon you shall hear a hog grunt, a calf bleat, and an ass bray,
Because it is Saint Peter's holiday.

      Re-enter all the FRIARS *to sing the Dirge*

1st Friar. Come, brethren, let's about our business with good devotion.

They sing:

Cursed be he that stole away his Holiness' meat from the
    table! *Maledicat Dominus!* [5]
Cursed be he that struck his Holiness a blow on the face!
    Maledicat Dominus!
Cursed be he that took Friar Sandelo a blow on the pate!
    Maledicat Dominus!
Cursed be he that disturbeth our holy dirge! *Maledicat*
    Dominus!
Cursed be he that took away his Holiness' wine! *Maledicat*
    Dominus! Et omnes sancti! [6] *Amen!*

[MEPHISTOPHILIS *and* FAUSTUS beat the FRIARS,
and fling fireworks among them: and so exeunt.]

Enter CHORUS

Chorus. When Faustus had with pleasure ta'en the view
Of rarest things, and royal courts of kings,
He stay'd his course, and so returned home;
Where such as bear his absence but with grief,
I mean his friends, and near'st companions,
Did gratulate his safety with kind words,
And in their conference of what befell,
Touching his journey through the world and air,
They put forth questions of Astrology,
Which Faustus answer'd with such learned skill,
As they admir'd and wond'red at his wit.
Now is his fame spread forth in every land;
Amongst the rest the Emperor is one,
Carolus the Fifth, at whose palace now
Faustus is feasted 'mongst his noblemen.
What there he did in trial of his art,

I leave untold—your eyes shall see perform'd. [*Exit.*]

[1] Treves.
[2] Virgil, who was reputed a magician in the Middle Ages, was buried at Naples.
[3] "A particular set of notes on the trumpet or cornet, different from a flourish."—*Nares.*
[4] If.
[5] "May the Lord curse him."
[6] "And all the saints."

Scene VIII

[An Inn-yard.]
Enter ROBIN *the Ostler with a book in his hand*

Robin. O, this is admirable! here I ha' stolen one of Dr.
Faustus' conjuring books, and i' faith I mean to search
come circles for my own use. Now will I make all the
maidens in our parish dance at my pleasure, stark naked
before me; and so by that means I shall see more than
e'er I felt or saw yet.

Enter RALPH *calling* ROBIN

Ralph. Robin, prithee come away; there's a gentleman
tarries to have his horse, and he would have his things
rubb'd and made clean. He keeps such a chafing with
my mistress about it; and she has sent me to look thee
out; prithee come away.

Robin. Keep out, keep out, or else you are blown up; you
are dismemb'red, Ralph: keep out, for I am about a
roaring piece of work.

Ralph. Come, what dost thou with that same book? Thou
canst not read.

Robin. Yes, my master and mistress shall find that I can
read, he for his forehead, she for her private study; she's
born to bear with me, or else my art fails.

Ralph. Why, Robin, what book is that?

Robin. What book! Why, the most intolerable book for conjuring that e'er was invented by any brimstone devil.

Ralph. Canst thou conjure with it?

Robin. I can do all these things easily with it: first, I can make thee drunk with ippocras [1] at any tabern [2] in Europe for nothing; that's one of my conjuring works.

Ralph. Our Master Parson says that's nothing.

Robin. True, Ralph; and more, Ralph, if thou hast any mind to Nan Spit, our kitchenmaid, then turn her and wind her to thy own use as often as thou wilt, and at midnight.

Ralph. O brave Robin, shall I have Nan Spit, and to mine own use? On that condition I'll feed thy devil with horsebread as long as he lives, of free cost.

Robin. No more, sweet Ralph: let's go and make clean our boots, which lie foul upon our hands, and then to our conjuring in the Devil's name. [*Exeunt.*]

[1] Wine mixed with sugar and spices.
[2] Tavern.

Scene IX

[*An Inn.*]
Enter ROBIN *and* RALPH *with a silver goblet.*

Robin. Come, Ralph, did not I tell thee we were for ever
made by this Doctor Faustus' book? *Ecce signum*, [1]
here's a simple purchase [2] for horsekeepers; our
horses shall eat not hay as long as this lasts.

Enter the VINTNER

Ralph. But, Robin, here come the vintner.

Robin. Hush! I'll gull him supernaturally.
Drawer, I hope all is paid: God be with you. Come, Ralph.

Vint. Soft, sir; a word with you. I must yet have a goblet
paid from you, ere you go.

Robin. I, a goblet, Ralph; I, a goblet! I scorn you, and you
are but a, [3] &c. I, a goblet! search me.

Vint. I mean so, sir, with your favour. [*Searches him.*]

Robin. How say you now?

Vint. I must say somewhat to your fellow. You, sir!

Ralph. Me, sir! me, sir! search your fill. [VINTNER
searches him.] Now, sir, you may be ashamed to burden
honest men with a matter of truth.

Vint. Well, t'one of you hath this goblet about you.

Robin. You lie, drawer, 'tis afore me. [*Aside.*] Sirrah you, I'll teach ye to impeach honest men;—stand by;—I'll scour you for a goblet!—stand aside you had best, I charge you in the name of Belzebub. Look to the goblet, Ralph. [*Aside to* RALPH.]

Vint. What mean you, sirrah?

Robin. I'll tell you what I mean. [*Reads from a book.*] *Sanctobulorum. Periphrasticon*—Nay, I'll tickle you, vintner. Look to the goblet, Ralph. [*Aside to* RALPH.] *Polypragmos Belseborams framanto pacostiphos tostu, Mephistophilis, &c.* [*Reads.*]

Enter MEPHISTOPHILIS, *sets squibs at their backs,* [*and then exit*]. *They run about*

Vint. O nomine Domini! [4] what meanest thou, Robin? Thou hast no goblet.

Ralph. Peccatum peccatorum! [5] Here's thy goblet, good vintner. [*Gives the goblet to* VINTNER, *who exit.*]

Robin. Misericordia pro nobis! [6] What shall I do? Good Devil, forgive me now, and I'll never rob thy library more.

Re-enter MEPHISTOPHILIS

Meph. Monarch of hell, under whose black survey
Great potentates do kneel with awful fear,
Upon whose altars thousand souls do lie,
How am I vexed with these villains' charms?
From Constantinople am I hither come

Only for pleasure of these damned slaves.

Robin. How from Constantinople? You have had a great journey. Will you take sixpence in your purse to pay for you supper, and begone?

Meph. Well, villains, for your presumption, I transform thee into an ape, and thee into a dog; and so begone. [*Exit.*]

Robin. How, into an ape? That's brave! I'll have fine sport with the boys. I'll get nuts and apples enow.

Ralph. And I must be a dog.

Robin. I'faith thy head will never be out of the pottage pot. [*Exeunt.*]

[1] "Behold a sign."
[2] Gain.
[3] The abuse was left to the actor's inventiveness.
[4] "In the name of the Lord."
[5] "Sin of sins."
[6] "Mercy on us."

Scene X

[The Court of the Emperor.]
Enter EMPEROR, FAUSTUS, *and a* KNIGHT *with
attendants*

Emp. Master Doctor Faustus, I have heard strange report of
thy knowledge in the black art, how that none in my
empire nor in the whole world can compare with thee
for the rare effects of magic; they say thou hast a
familiar spirit, by whom thou canst accomplish what
thou list. This therefore is my request, that thou let me
see some proof of thy skill, that mine eyes may be
witnesses to confirm what mine ears have heard
reported; and here I swear to thee by the honour of
mine imperial crown, that, whatever thou doest, thou
shalt be no ways prejudiced or endamaged.

Knight. I'faith he looks much like a conjuror. [*Aside.*]

Faust. My gracious sovereign, though I must confess
myself far inferior to the report men have published,
and nothing answerable [1] to the honour of your
imperial majesty, yet for that love and duty binds me
thereunto, I am content to do whatsoever your majesty
shall command me.

Emp. Then, Doctor Faustus, mark what I shall say.
As I was sometime solitary set
Within my closet, sundry thoughts arose
About the honour of mine ancestors,
How they had won by prowess such exploits,
Got such riches, subdued so many kingdoms
As we that do succeed, or they that shall

Hereafter possess our throne, shall
(I fear me) ne'er attain to that degree
Of high renown and great authority;
Amongst which kings is Alexander the Great,
Chief spectacle of the world's pre-eminence,
The bright shining of whose glorious acts
Lightens the world with his [2] reflecting beams,
As when I heard but motion [3] made of him
It grieves my soul I never saw the man.
If therefore thou by cunning of thine art
Canst raise this man from hollow vaults below,
Where lies entomb'd this famous conqueror,
And bring with him his beauteous paramour,
Both in their right shapes, gesture, and attire
They us'd to wear during their time of life,
Thou shalt both satisfy my just desire,
And give me cause to praise thee whilst I live.

Faust. My gracious lord, I am ready to accomplish your
request so far forth as by art, and power of my Spirit, I
am able to perform.

Knight. I'faith that's just nothing at all. [*Aside.*]

Faust. But, if it like your Grace, it is not in my ability to
present before your eyes the true substantial bodies of
those two deceased princes, which long since are
consumed to dust.

Knight. Ay, marry, Master Doctor, now there's a sign of
grace in you, when you will confess the truth. [*Aside.*]

Faust. But such spirits as can lively resemble Alexander
and his paramour shall appear before your Grace in that
manner that they [best] live in, in their most flourishing

estate; which I doubt not shall sufficiently content your imperial majesty.

Emp. Go to, Master Doctor, let me see them presently.

Knight. Do you hear, Master Doctor? You bring Alexander and his paramour before the Emperor!

Faust. How then, sir?

Knight. I'faith that's as true as Diana turn'd me to a stag!

Faust. No, sir, but when Actæon died, he left the horns for you. Mephistophilis, begone. [*Exit Mephisto.*]

Knight. Nay, an you go to conjuring. I'll begone. [*Exit.*]

Faust. I'll meet with you anon for interrupting me so. Here they are, my gracious lord.

Re-enter MEPHISTOPHILIS *with* [SPIRITS *in the shape of*] ALEXANDER *and his* PARAMOUR

Emp. Master Doctor, I heard this lady while she liv'd had a wart or mole in her neck: how shall I know whether it be so or no?

Faust. Your Highness may boldly go and see.

Emp. Sure these are no spirits, but the true substantial bodies of those two deceased princes. [*Exeunt* Spirits.]

Faust. Will't please your highness now to send for the knight that was so pleasant with me here of late?

Emp. One of you call him forth. [*Exit* Attendant.]

Re-enter the KNIGHT *with a pair of horns on his head*

How now, sir knight! why I had thought thou had'st been a bachelor, but now I see thou hast a wife, that not only gives thee horns, but makes thee wear them. Feel on thy head.

Knight. Thou damned wretch and execrable dog,
Bred in the concave of some monstrous rock,
How darest thou thus abuse a gentleman?
Villain, I say, undo what thou hast done!

Faust. O, not so fast, sir; there's no haste; but, good, are you rememb'red how you crossed me in my conference with the Emperor? I think I have met with you for it.

Emp. Good Master Doctor, at my entreaty release him; he hath done penance sufficient.

Faust. My gracious lord, not so much for the injury he off'red me here in your presence, as to delight you with some mirth, hath Faustus worthily requited this injurious knight; which, being all I desire, I am content to release him of his horns: and, sir knight, hereafter speak well of scholars. Mephistophilis, transform him straight. [MEPHISTOPHILIS *removes the horns*.] Now, my good lord, having done my duty I humbly take my leave.

Emp. Farewell, Master Doctor; yet, ere you go,
Expect from me a bounteous reward. [*Exeunt*.]

[1] Proportionate.

60

[2] Its.
[3] Mention.

Scene XI

[A Green; afterwards the House of Faustus]
[Enter FAUSTUS *and* MEPHISTOPHILIS]

Faust. Now, Mephistophilis, the restless course
That Time doth run with calm and silent foot,
Short'ning my days and thread of vital life,
Calls for the payment of my latest years;
Therefore, sweet Mephistophilis, let us
Make haste to Wittenberg.

Meph. What, will you go on horseback or on foot?

Faust. Nay, till I'm past this fair and pleasant green, I'll
walk on foot.

Enter a HORSE-COURSER

Horse-C. I have been all this day seeking one Master
Fustian: mass, see where he is! God save you, Master
Doctor!

Faust. What, horse-courser! You are well met.

Horse-C. Do you hear, sir? I have brought you forty dollars
for your horse.

Faust. I cannot sell him so: if thou likest him for fifty take
him.

Horse-C. Alas, sir, I have no more.—I pray you speak for
me.

Meph. I pray you let him have him: he is an honest fellow, and he has a great charge, neither wife nor child.

Faust. Well, come, give me your money. [HORSE-COURSER *gives* FAUSTUS *the money*.] My boy will deliver him to you. But I must tell you one thing before you have him; ride him not into the water at any hand.

Horse-C. Why, sir, will he not drink of all waters?

Faust. O yes, he will drink of all waters, but ride him not into the water: ride him over hedge or ditch, or where thou wilt, but not into the water.

Horse-C. Well, sir.—Now I am made man for ever. I'll not leave my horse for forty. If he had but the quality of hey-ding-ding, hey-ding-ding, I'd made a brave living on him: he has a buttock as slick as an eel. [Aside.] Well, God b' wi' ye, sir, your boy will deliver him me: but hark you, sir; if my horse be sick or ill at ease, if I bring his water to you, you'll tell me what it is.

Faust. Away, you villain; what, dost think I am a horse-doctor?

Exit HORSE-COURSER.

What art thou, Faustus, but a man condemn'd to die?
Thy fatal time doth draw to final end;
Despair doth drive distrust unto my thoughts:
Confound these passions with a quiet sleep:
Tush, Christ did call the thief upon the cross;
Then rest thee, Faustus, quiet in conceit. [*Sleeps in his chair*.]

Re-enter HORSE-COURSER, *all wet, crying*

Horse-C. Alas, alas! Doctor Fustian quotha? Mass, Doctor Lopus [1] was never such a doctor. Has given me a purgation has purg'd me of forty dollars; I shall never see them more. But yet, like an ass as I was, I would not be ruled by him, for he bade me I should ride him into no water. Now I, thinking my horse had had some rare quality that he would not have had me known of, I, like a venturous youth rid him into the deep pond at the town's end. I was no sooner in the middle of the pond, but my horse vanished away, and I sat upon a bottle of hay, never so near drowning in my life. But I'll seek out my Doctor, and have my forty dollars again, or I'll make it the dearest horse!—O, yonder is his snipper-snapper.—Do you hear? You hey-pass, [2] where's your master?

Meph. Why, sir, what would you? You cannot speak with him.

Horse-C. But I will speak with him.

Meph. Why, he's fast asleep. Come some other time.

Horse-C. I'll speak with him now, or I'll break his glass windows about his ears.

Meph. I tell thee he has not slept this eight nights.

Horse-C. An he have not slept this eight weeks, I'll speak with him.

Meph. See where he is, fast asleep.

Horse-C. Ay, this is he. God save you, Master Doctor! Master Doctor, Master Doctor Fustian!—Forty dollars, forty dollars for a bottle of hay!

Meph. Why, thou seest he hears thee not.

Horse-C. So ho, ho!—so ho, ho! [*Hollas in his ear.*] No, will you not wake? I'll make you wake ere I go. [*Pulls* FAUSTUS *by the leg, and pulls it away.*] Alas, I am undone! What shall I do?

Faust. O my leg, my leg! Help, Mephistophilis! call the officers. My leg, my leg!

Meph. Come, villain, to the constable.

Horse-C. O lord, sir, let me go, and I'll give you forty dollars more.

Meph. Where be they?

Horse-C. I have none about me. Come to my ostry [3] and I'll give them you.

Meph. Begone quickly. [HORSE-COURSER *runs away.*]

Faust. What, is he gone? Farewell he! Faustus has his leg again, and the horse-courser, I take it, a bottle of hay for his labour. Well, this trick shall cost him forty dollars more.

Enter WAGNER

How now, Wagner, what's the news with thee?

Wag. Sir, the Duke of Vanholt doth earnestly entreat your company.

Faust. The Duke of Vanholt! an honourable gentleman, to whom I must be no niggard of my cunning. Come, Mephistophilis, let's away to him. [*Exeunt.*]

[1] Dr. Lopez, physician to Queen Elizabeth, was hanged in 1594 on the charge of conspiring to poison the Queen.
[2] A juggler's term, like "presto, fly!" Hence applied to the juggler himself.—*Bullen.*
[3] Inn.

Scene XII

[The Court of the Duke of Vanholt.]
Enter the DUKE *[of* VANHOLT], *the* DUCHESS,
FAUSTUS, *and* MEPHISTOPHILIS

Duke. Believe me, Master Doctor, this merriment hath much pleased me.

Faust. My gracious lord, I am glad it contents you so well.—But it may be, madam, you take no delight in this. I have heard that great-bellied women do long for some dainties or other. What is it, madam? Tell me, and you shall have it.

Duchess. Thanks, good Master Doctor; and for I see your courteous intent to pleasure me, I will not hide from you the thing my heart desires; and were it now summer, as it is January and the dead time of the winter, I would desire no better meat than a dish of ripe grapes.

Faust. Alas, madam, that's nothing! Mephistophilis, begone. [*Exit* MEPHISTOPHILIS.] Were it a greater thing than this, so it would content you, you should have it.

Re-enter MEPHISTOPHILIS *with the grapes*

Here they be, madam; wilt please you taste on them?

Duke. Believe me, Master Doctor, this makes me wonder above the rest, that being in the dead time of winter, and in the month of January, how you should come by these grapes.

Faust. If it like your Grace, the year is divided into two circles over the whole world, that, when it is here winter with us, in the contrary circle it is summer with them, as in India, Saba, and farther countries in the East; and by means of a swift spirit that I have I had them brought hither, as ye see.—How do you like them, madam; be they good?

Duchess. Believe me, Master Doctor, they be the best grapes that I e'er tasted in my life before.

Faust. I am glad they content you so, madam.

Duke. Come, madam, let us in, where you must well reward this learned man for the great kindness he hath show'd to you.

Duchess. And so I will, my lord; and, whilst I live, rest beholding for this courtesy.

Faust. I humbly thank your Grace.

Duke. Come, Master Doctor, follow us and receive your reward. [*Exeunt.*]

Scene XIII

[A room in Faustus' House.]
Enter WAGNER

Wag. I think my master shortly means to die,
For he hath given to me all his goods;
And yet, methinks, if that death were so near,
He would not banquet and carouse and swill
Amongst the students, as even now he doth,
Who are at supper with such belly-cheer
As Wagner ne'er beheld in all his life.
See where they come! Belike the feast is ended.

Enter FAUSTUS, *with two or three* SCHOLARS [*and*
MEPHISTOPHILIS]

1st Schol. Master Doctor Faustus, since our conference
about fair ladies, which was the beautifullest in all the
world, we have determined with ourselves that Helen of
Greece was the admirablest lady that ever lived:
therefore, Master Doctor, if you will do us that favour,
as to let us see that peerless dame of Greece, whom all
the world admires for majesty, we should think
ourselves much beholding unto you.

Faust. Gentlemen,
For that I know your friendship is unfeigned,
And Faustus' custom is not to deny
The just requests of those that wish him well,
You shall behold that peerless dame of Greece,
No otherways for pomp and majesty
Than when Sir Paris cross'd the seas with her,
And brought the spoils to rich Dardania.

Be silent, then, for danger is in words. [*Music sounds, and*
    HELEN *passeth over the stage*.]

2nd Schol. Too simple is my wit to tell her praise,
Whom all the world admires for majesty.

3rd Schol. No marvel though the angry Greeks pursued
With ten years' war the rape of such a queen,
Whose heavenly beauty passeth all compare.

1st Schol. Since we have seen the pride of Nature's works,
And only paragon of excellence,
Let us depart; and for this glorious deed
Happy and blest be Faustus evermore.

Faustus. Gentlemen, farewell—the same I wish to you.
    [*Exeunt* SCHOLARS *and* WAGNER].

Enter an OLD MAN

Old Man. Ah, Doctor Faustus, that I might prevail
To guide thy steps unto the way of life,
By which sweet path thou may'st attain the goal
That shall conduct thee to celestial rest!
Break heart, drop blood, and mingle it with tears,
Tears falling from repentant heaviness
Of thy most vile and loathsome filthiness,
The stench whereof corrupts the inward soul
With such flagitious crimes of heinous sins
As no commiseration may expel,
But mercy, Faustus, of thy Saviour sweet,
Whose blood alone must wash away thy guilt.

Faust. Where art thou, Faustus? Wretch, what hast thou
    done?

Damn'd art thou, Faustus, damn'd; despair and die!
Hell calls for right, and with a roaring voice
Says "Faustus! come! thine hour is [almost] come!"
And Faustus [now] will come to do the right.
    [MEPHISTOPHILIS *gives him a dagger*.]

Old Man. Ah stay, good Faustus, stay thy desperate steps!
I see an angel hovers o'er thy head,
And, with a vial full of precious grace,
Offers to pour the same into thy soul:
Then call for mercy, and avoid despair.

Faust. Ah, my sweet friend, I feel
Thy words do comfort my distressed soul.
Leave me a while to ponder on my sins.

Old Man. I go, sweet Faustus, but with heavy cheer,
Fearing the ruin of thy hopeless soul. [*Exit.*]

Faust. Accursed Faustus, where is mercy now?
I do repent; and yet I do despair;
Hell strives with grace for conquest in my breast:
What shall I do to shun the snares of death?

Meph. Thou traitor, Faustus, I arrest thy soul
For disobedience to my sovereign lord;
Revolt, or I'll in piecemeal tear thy flesh.

Faust. Sweet Mephistophilis, entreat thy lord
To pardon my unjust presumption.
And with my blood again I will confirm
My former vow I made to Lucifer.

Meph. Do it then quickly, with unfeigned heart,

Lest greater danger do attend thy drift. [FAUSTUS *stabs his arm and writes on a paper with his blood.*]

Faust. Torment, sweet friend, that base and crooked age,
   [1]
That durst dissuade me from my Lucifer,
With greatest torments that our hell affords.

Meph. His faith is great, I cannot touch his soul;
But what I may afflict his body with
I will attempt, which is but little worth.

Faust. One thing, good servant, let me crave of thee,
To glut the longing of my heart's desire,—
That I might have unto my paramour
That heavenly Helen, Which I saw of late,
Whose sweet embracings may extinguish clean
These thoughts that do dissuade me from my vow,
And keep mine oath I made to Lucifer.

Meph. Faustus, this or what else thou shalt desire
Shall be perform'd in twinkling of an eye.

Re-enter HELEN

Faust. Was this the face that launched a thousand ships
And burnt the topless [2] towers of Ilium?
Sweet Helen, make me immortal with a kiss. [*Kisses her.*]
Her lips suck forth my soul; see where it flies!—
Come, Helen, come, give me my soul again.
Here will I dwell, for Heaven is in these lips,
And all is dross that is not Helena. [*Enter* OLD MAN.]
I will be Paris, and for love of thee,
Instead of Troy, shall Wittenberg be sack'd;
And I will combat with weak Menelaus,

And wear thy colours on my plumed crest;
Yea, I will wound Achilles in the heel,
And then return to Helen for a kiss.
Oh, thou art fairer than the evening air
Clad in the beauty of a thousand stars;
Brighter art thou than flaming Jupiter
When he appear'd to hapless Semele:
More lovely than the monarch of the sky
In wanton Arethusa's azured arms:
And none but thou shalt be my paramour. [*Exeunt.*]

Old Man. Accursed Faustus, miserable man,
That from thy soul exclud'st the grace of Heaven,
And fly'st the throne of his tribunal seat!

Enter DEVILS

Satan begins to sift me with his pride:
As in this furnace God shall try my faith,
My faith, vile hell, shall triumph over thee.
Ambitious fiends! see how the heavens smiles
At your repulse, and laughs your state to scorn!
Hence, hell! for hence I fly unto my God. [*Exeunt on one
    side* DEVILS, *on the other*, OLD MAN].

[1] Old man.
[2] Unsurpassed in height.

Scene XIV

[*The Same.*]
Enter FAUSTUS *with* SCHOLARS

Faust. Ah, gentlemen!

1st Schol. What ails Faustus?

Faust. Ah, my sweet chamber-fellow, had I lived with thee, then had I lived still! but now I die eternally. Look, comes he not, comes he not?

2nd Schol. What means Faustus?

3rd Schol. Belike he is grown into some sickness by being over solitary.

1st Schol. If it be so, we'll have physicians to cure him. 'Tis but a surfeit. Never fear, man.

Faust. A surfeit of deadly sin that hath damn'd both body and soul.

2nd Schol. Yet, Faustus, look up to Heaven; remember God's mercies are infinite.

Faust. But Faustus' offenses can never be pardoned: the serpent that tempted Eve may be sav'd, but not Faustus. Ah, gentlemen, hear me with patience, and tremble not at my speeches! Though my heart pants and quivers to remember that I have been a student here these thirty years, oh, would I had never seen Wittenberg, never read book! And what wonders I have done, All

Germany can witness, yea, the world; for which Faustus hath lost both Germany and the world, yea Heaven itself, Heaven, the seat of God, the throne of the blessed, the kingdom of joy; and must remain in hell for ever, hell, ah, hell, for ever! Sweet friends! what shall become of Faustus being in hell for ever?

3rd Schol. Yet, Faustus, call on God.

Faust. On God, whom Faustus hath abjur'd! on God, whom Faustus hath blasphemed! Ah, my God, I would weep, but the Devil draws in my tears. Gush forth blood instead of tears! Yea, life and soul! Oh, he stays my tongue! I would lift up my hands, but see, they hold them, they hold them!

All. Who, Faustus?

Faust. Lucifer and Mephistophilis. Ah, gentlemen, I gave them my soul for my cunning!

All. God forbid!

Faust. God forbade it indeed; but Faustus hath done it. For vain pleasure of twenty-four years hath Faustus lost eternal joy and felicity. I writ them a bill with mine own blood: the date is expired; the time will come, and he will fetch me.

1st Schol. Why did not Faustus tell us of this before, that divines might have pray'd for thee?

Faust. Oft have I thought to have done so; but the Devil threat'ned to tear me in pieces if I nam'd God; to fetch both body and soul if I once gave ear to divinity: and

now 'tis too late. Gentlemen, away! lest you perish with
me.

2nd Schol. Oh, what shall we do to save Faustus?

Faust. Talk not of me, but save yourselves, and depart.

3rd Schol. God will strengthen me. I will stay with Faustus.

1st Schol. Tempt not God, sweet friend; but let us into the
next room, and there pray for him.

Faust. Ay, pray for me, pray for me! and what noise soever
ye hear, come not unto me, for nothing can rescue me.

2nd Schol. Pray thou, and we will pray that God may have
mercy upon thee.

Faust. Gentlemen, farewell! If I live till morning I'll visit
you: if not—Faustus is gone to hell.

All. Faustus, farewell! [*Exeunt* SCHOLARS. *The clock
strikes eleven.*]

Faust. Ah, Faustus,
Now hast thou but one bare hour to live,
And then thou must be damn'd perpetually!
Stand still, you ever-moving spheres of Heaven,
That time may cease, and midnight never come;
Fair Nature's eye, rise, rise again and make
Perpetual day; or let this hour be but
A year, a month, a week, a natural day,
That Faustus may repent and save his soul!
O lente, lente, curite noctis equi. [1]
The stars move still, [2] time runs, the clock will strike,

The Devil will come, and Faustus must be damn'd.
O, I'll leap up to my God! Who pulls me down?
See, see where Christ's blood streams in the firmament!
One drop would save my soul—half a drop: ah, my Christ!
Ah, rend not my heart for naming of my Christ!
Yet will I call on him: O spare me, Lucifer!—
Where is it now? 'Tis gone; and see where God
Stretcheth out his arm, and bends his ireful brows!
Mountain and hills come, come and fall on me,
And hide me from the heavy wrath of God!
No! no!
Then will I headlong run into the earth;
Earth gape! O no, it will not harbour me!
You stars that reign'd at my nativity,
Whose influence hath alloted death and hell,
Now draw up Faustus like a foggy mist
Into the entrails of yon labouring clouds,
That when they vomit forth into the air,
My limbs may issue from their smoky mouths,
So that my soul may but ascend to Heaven. [*The watch
    strikes the half hour*].
Ah, half the hour is past! 'Twill all be past anon!
O God!
If thou wilt not have mercy on my soul,
Yet for Christ's sake whose blood hath ransom'd me,
Impose some end to my incessant pain;
Let Faustus live in hell a thousand years—
A hundred thousand, and—at last—be sav'd!
O, no end is limited to damned souls!
Why wert thou not a creature wanting soul?
Or why is this immortal that thou hast?
Ah, Pythogoras' metempsychosis! were that true,
This soul should fly from me, and I be chang'd
Unto some brutish beast! All beasts are happy,
For when they die,

Their souls are soon dissolv'd in elements;
But mine must live, still to be plagu'd in hell.
Curst be the parents that engend'red me!
No, Faustus: curse thyself: curse Lucifer
That hath depriv'd thee of the joys of Heaven. [*The clock striketh twelve.*]
O, it strikes, it strikes! Now, body, turn to air,
Or Lucifer will bear thee quick to hell. [*Thunder and lightning.*]
O soul, be chang'd into little water-drops,
And fall into the ocean—ne'er be found.
My God! my God! look not so fierce on me! [*Enter DEVILS.*]
Adders and serpents, let me breathe awhile!
Ugly hell, gape not! come not, Lucifer!
I'll burn my books!—Ah Mephistophilis! [*Exeunt DEVILS with FAUSTUS.*]

Enter CHORUS

Cho. Cut is the branch that might have grown full straight,
And burned is Apollo's laurel bough,
That sometime grew within this learned man.
Faustus is gone; regard his hellish fall,
Whose fiendful fortune may exhort the wise
Only to wonder at unlawful things,
Whose deepness doth entice such forward wits
To practise more than heavenly power permits. [*Exit.*]

[1] "Run softly, softly, horses of the night."—Ovid's *Amores*, i, 13.
[2] Without ceasing.

THE END